The Bill of Rights

The Bill of Rights

Dennis Brindell Fradin

 **Marshall Cavendish**
Benchmark

New York

Consultant:

Michael Fradin, Attorney at Law

Marshall Cavendish Benchmark
99 White Plains Road
Tarrytown, New York 10591-5502
www.marshallcavendish.us

Text and maps copyright © 2009 by Marshall Cavendish Corporation
Map by XNR Productions

All Internet sites were available and accurate when sent to press.

Library of Congress Cataloging-in-Publication Data
Fradin, Dennis B.
The Bill of Rights / by Dennis Brindell Fradin.
p. cm. — (Turning points in U.S. history)
Summary: "Covers the Bill of Rights as a watershed document in U.S.
history, influencing social, economic, and political policies that shaped
the nation's future"—Provided by publisher.
Includes bibliographical references and index.
ISBN 978-0-7614-3009-4
1. Civil rights—United States—History. 2. Constitutional history—United
States. 3. United States. Constitution. 1st-10th Amendments. I. Title.
KF4749.F665 2009
342.7308'5—dc22
2007030449

Photo research by Connie Gardner

Cover photo by Robert L. Wollenberg/Digital Railroad
Cover Photo: People view important U.S. documents in the Rotunda of the National Archives in Washington, D.C.
Title Page: In Washington, D.C., students attend a free speech rally outside the Supreme Court building.

The photographs in this book are used by permission and through the courtesy of: *Corbis*: Holly Riley, 3, 34; Museum of the City of New York, 6; Joseph
Sohm, Visions of America, 8, 22; Bettmann, 10, 14, 24, 28, 42-43; Jodi Hilton, 36; *Getty Images:* Hulton Archives, 12; AFP/Hector Mata, 33; *The Granger
Collection:* 13, 30; *NorthWind Picture Archives:* 16, 21, 26

Editor: Deborah Grahame
Publisher: Michelle Bisson
Art Director: Anahid Hamparian

Printed in Malaysia
1 3 5 6 4 2

Contents

After crossing the Atlantic Ocean in the *Mayflower*, the Pilgrims landed at Plymouth, Massachusetts, in December 1620.

CHAPTER ONE

A Nation Begins

Between 1607 and 1733 England settled or took over a string of **colonies** along the East Coast of North America. They were called England's thirteen American colonies.

For many years the colonists had few complaints about English rule. Then, in the 1760s, the colonists began to **rebel**. One reason was that England taxed its colonies heavily. Another was that the colonists felt ready to rule themselves.

In 1775 the Revolutionary War broke out between the colonists and England. The next year, on July 4, 1776, the new American

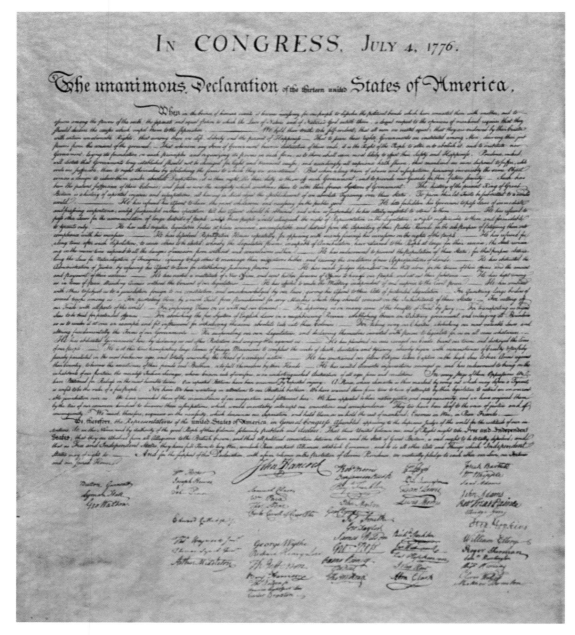

A copy of the original Declaration of Independence, signed by all fifty-six members of Congress. It has been called the "best-loved document in U.S. history."

government issued the Declaration of Independence. This document announced that the thirteen colonies were now the United States of America. The Declaration created a new country, so it was nicknamed the nation's birth certificate.

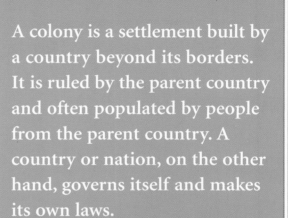

Colony or Country?

A colony is a settlement built by a country beyond its borders. It is ruled by the parent country and often populated by people from the parent country. A country or nation, on the other hand, governs itself and makes its own laws.

Colonists in blue confront the British redcoats during the Battle of Concord, marking the beginning of the Revolutionary War.

CHAPTER TWO

The Constitution
of the United States

The Americans won the Revolutionary War in 1783. Now independence was more than a word on paper. Even England recognized the United States as a separate nation.

It appeared that the new country would not last long, though. There was a huge problem. The U.S. government, called the Continental **Congress**, was too weak.

To begin, there was no president to lead the nation. The country also lacked a permanent **capital**. This meant that lawmakers had to move from city to city to go to government meetings. In addition, the Continental

Congress had no **authority** to collect taxes. With little money, the government could not pay its bills.

The new government had many more weaknesses. There were no national courts to settle major conflicts. The country also lacked a national money system. Each state printed its own money, so it was difficult to do business across state boundaries. Finally, the young country had only a tiny army. It could not even defend itself properly.

This wallet belonged to a colonial soldier and contains paper money and coins used as New Jersey's currency in the 1750s.

By 1786 things were not looking good for the United States. George Washington had led the United States to victory in the Revolutionary War. Now he saw little future for the country. In a letter to his fellow Virginian James Madison, Washington wrote that the nation must make "some **alteration** in our political **creed**." Otherwise, Washington believed, the government would fall apart.

Other well-known Americans agreed. In the spring of 1787 American leaders gathered in Philadelphia, Pennsylvania. Their job was to strengthen the U.S. government. One state, Rhode Island, refused to participate. As the smallest state, Little Rhody was afraid of being swallowed up by a strong **federal** government. The other twelve states sent **delegates** to the meeting.

The Constitutional **Convention** began on May 25, 1787. For four months the delegates worked on a written framework of government for the nation. They called it the **Constitution** of the United States. The Constitution established a federal government with three branches. The legislative branch, composed of the House of Representatives and the Senate, would make laws. The executive branch, headed by the

Independence Hall, also known as the Philadelphia State House, as it appeared in 1776

This painting shows the delegates assembled to sign the U.S. Constitution, with George Washington leading the group.

president, would make sure laws were carried out. The judicial branch, or courts, would make important legal decisions.

The Constitution solved many of the nation's problems. One part called for the creation of a permanent U.S. capital. It turned out to be Washington, D.C. The document also gave the government the power to collect taxes, to establish armies, and to make its own money.

What if Americans wanted to amend, or change, the Constitution? The delegates had the answer. Amendments could be added to the Constitution with the approval of three-fourths of the states.

The Constitution was written, but it still had to be put into effect. The states would hold conventions of their own to consider the new Constitution. If nine of the thirteen states ratified (approved) it, the Constitution would become "the supreme law of the land."

The Constitutional Convention ended on September 17, 1787. That day thirty-nine delegates signed the Constitution. One of them, James Madison, had done so much to create it that he became known as the Father of the Constitution.

Three delegates—Edmund Randolph and George Mason of Virginia and Elbridge Gerry of Massachusetts—refused to sign the Constitution. A main **objection** was that the Constitution lacked a bill of rights—a section protecting certain basic rights of citizens. The three men's refusal to sign the Constitution was a hint of what lay ahead.

New Yorkers celebrated the adoption of the Constitution with a parade on Wall Street. The "Ship of State" honored Alexander Hamilton, the state's delegate to the Constitutional Convention.

CHAPTER THREE

The Call for a Bill of Rights

In late 1787 the states began holding conventions. Each state had to decide whether or not to ratify the Constitution. State after state approved the document. On June 21, 1788, New Hampshire became the ninth state to approve the Constitution. With a two-thirds **majority**, the document could now go into effect. Shortly afterward Virginia and New York added their approval. Eleven of the thirteen states had joined together under the Constitution.

Approval did not come easy, though. The Constitution probably had about as many **opponents** as supporters. The vote was often close at the states' ratifying conventions. For example, Virginia's leaders approved

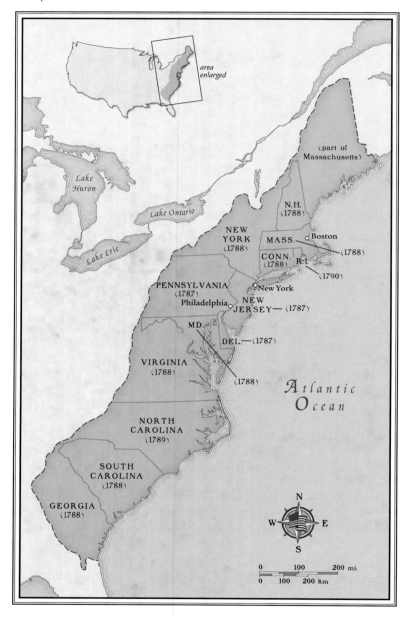

the Constitution by only an 89–79 vote. New York's vote was even closer, at 30–27. If just two votes had gone the other way, New York would have rejected the document.

The Constitution's opponents believed the central government would become too powerful. Like Elbridge Gerry, George Mason, and Edmund Randolph, many Americans wanted the Constitution to include a bill of rights. That way, no matter how powerful the government grew, certain basic rights of Americans would always be protected. Several states sent proposals for a bill of rights to Congress.

There was another problem. It appeared that two

This map shows the thirteen colonies and the dates each approved the Constitution.

Making the States

The thirteen colonies became known as states with the writing of the Declaration of Independence in 1776. But when Americans use the word *states* today, they mean states under the Constitution. On the day they ratified the Constitution, the former colonies became states in the modern sense. The following list shows when the thirteen former colonies approved the Constitution and achieved official statehood:

1. Delaware: Friday, December 7, 1787
2. Pennsylvania: Wednesday, December 12, 1787
3. New Jersey: Tuesday, December 18, 1787
4. Georgia: Wednesday, January 2, 1788
5. Connecticut: Wednesday, January 9, 1788
6. Massachusetts: Wednesday, February 6, 1788
7. Maryland: Monday, April 28, 1788
8. South Carolina: Friday, May 23, 1788
9. New Hampshire: Saturday, June 21, 1788
10. Virginia: Wednesday, June 25, 1788
11. New York: Saturday, July 26, 1788
12. North Carolina: Saturday, November 21, 1789
13. Rhode Island: Saturday, May 29, 1790

"Mister Mammoth"

At a time when the average man stood five feet six inches tall, Thomas Jefferson was six feet two. He was called "Tall Tom" as a young man. Among his many achievements besides writing the Declaration of Independence, he served as vice president of the United States from 1797 to 1801 and as the nation's third president from 1801 to 1809. He also designed the Virginia statehouse in Richmond, founded the University of Virginia, and was nicknamed "Mr. Mammoth" because he collected prehistoric bones.

states—North Carolina and Rhode Island—might never ratify the Constitution. Again, the lack of a bill of rights was the main roadblock. This was a serious situation. How could the country hold together if two states would not accept its basic framework of government?

At first, James Madison opposed adding a bill of rights to the Constitution. The Father of the Constitution considered it unnecessary. His close friend Thomas Jefferson helped convince him otherwise.

Jefferson, who was representing the United States in France at the time, exchanged letters with Madison. "I will now add what I do not like" about the Constitution, Jefferson wrote to Madison on December 20, 1787. "First the omission of a bill of rights. A bill of rights is what the people are **entitled** to against every government on Earth." On March 15, 1789, Jefferson wrote to Madison that a bill of rights would "brace up" the people's confidence in the federal government.

Jefferson's arguments helped change Madison's mind. By the spring of 1789, Madison favored the addition of a bill of rights to the Constitution.

Thomas Jefferson (1743–1826)

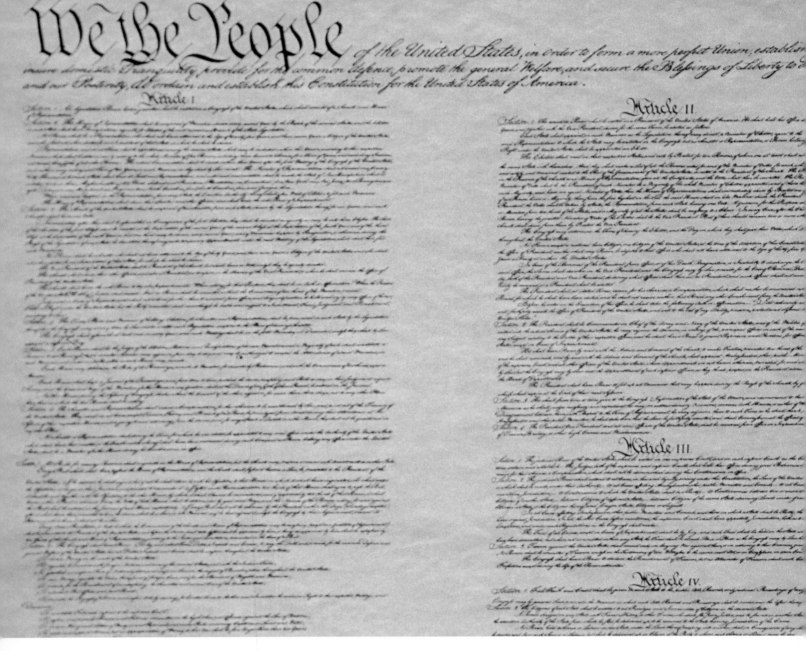

A copy of the original U.S. Constitution. The thirty-nine men who signed the document are called the Founding Fathers.

CHAPTER FOUR

Creating the Bill of Rights

When New Hampshire became the ninth state to ratify it, the U.S. Constitution went into effect. The country held elections to fill offices in the new government. The first elections for seats in the U.S. House of Representatives, or Congress, were held in 1788 and 1789. (Different states held elections at different times.) James Madison ran for a House seat in Virginia's election of early 1789. He made a campaign pledge. If elected, Madison would work to add a bill of rights to the Constitution. Madison won the election.

The House of Representatives began operating for the first time on April 1, 1789. Madison kept his campaign promise. On May 4, 1789, he made an announcement to his fellow congressmen. In a few weeks he would suggest amendments to the Constitution to safeguard citizens' rights.

Meanwhile, Madison had been writing a bill of rights. He researched many sources, such as old English laws and documents. He read state constitutions that guaranteed citizens' rights. He pored over more than two hundred amendments proposed by various states. Madison read newspapers to see which rights people were discussing around the country. Virginia's Declaration of Rights of 1776, drafted by George Mason, also influenced Madison.

Thomas Jefferson and other Virginia lawmakers are shown working on a document calling for freedom of religion, later one of the inspirations for the Bill of Rights.

After studying all these sources, Madison identified about twenty basic rights that most Americans wanted to protect. On June 8, 1789, he rose to speak in the House of Representatives. He declared that lawmakers must "provide those securities for liberty" that the people wanted. He then read aloud his list of basic rights.

The House of Representatives and the Senate approved Madison's bill of rights but reduced the number of amendments to twelve. These twelve proposed amendments were sent to President George Washington. He sent them on to the state legislatures for their approval.

The states rejected two of the amendments but approved the other ten. On November 20, 1789, New Jersey became the first state to ratify the Bill of Rights. Next came Maryland, North Carolina, South Carolina, New Hampshire, Delaware, New York, Pennsylvania, and Rhode Island. In November 1791, Vermont (which had become a state that March) gave its approval.

The big moment came in December, when Virginia ratified the bill. Virginia was the eleventh of the fourteen states to approve the Bill of Rights. The required three-fourths of the states had now granted their approval. On the day of Virginia's approval—December 15, 1791— the Bill of Rights became part of the Constitution of the United States.

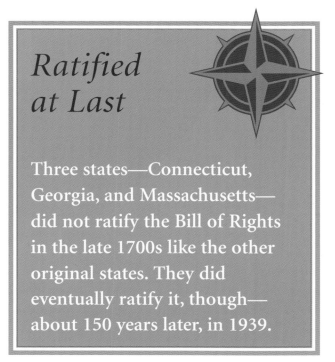

Ratified at Last

Three states—Connecticut, Georgia, and Massachusetts— did not ratify the Bill of Rights in the late 1700s like the other original states. They did eventually ratify it, though— about 150 years later, in 1939.

James Madison was a key figure at the Constitutional Convention of 1787. His notes tell us much about the event.

CHAPTER FIVE

"The Foundation of Our National Identity"

The Bill of Rights was largely the creation of one man. James Madison wrote the document. He also helped it gain acceptance in Congress. As a result, the Father of the Constitution earned another nickname. He also became known as the Father of the Bill of Rights.

The Bill of Rights was a turning point in U.S. history. The creation of the Bill of Rights helped make the Constitution more acceptable to North Carolina and Rhode Island. North Carolina ratified the Constitution on November 21, 1789. Rhode Island ratified it on May 29, 1790. Little Rhody was the last of the original states to approve the Constitution. Thanks partly to the Bill of Rights, all of the original thirteen states had banded together under the Constitution.

On December 15, 1941, people in New York City celebrated the 150th anniversary of the Bill of Rights.

The Bill of Rights also helped make the United States a special place to live. For more than two hundred years, Americans have taken great pride in their Bill of Rights. The amendment has helped define the United States as a country that protects basic rights such as freedom of religion, freedom of speech, and the right to a fair trial.

Warren E. Burger, chief justice of the U.S. Supreme Court from 1969

The Father of the Bill of Rights

James Madison (1751–1836), the oldest of twelve children, was born in Port Conway, Virginia. He grew up at Montpelier, his family's Virginia plantation. This remained his lifelong home. Madison was only five feet four inches tall and weighed just one hundred pounds. His voice was so quiet that people could barely hear him.

What made Madison special was his brilliant mind. As a young man he served in Virginia's revolutionary government and represented Virginia in the Continental Congress. Later he was the key figure in the creation of the U.S. Constitution and the Bill of Rights. From 1809 to 1817 he served as the fourth president of the United States. Madison lived to the age of eighty-five.

to 1986, summarized what the Constitution and the Bill of Rights mean to Americans:

> *We were the first people in history to found a nation on the basis of individual rights—a nation governed by "we the people." While many nations are based upon a common religion or ethnic heritage, or upon natural geographic frontiers, Americans have made individual rights the foundation of our national identity.*

Original copies of the Bill of Rights, as well as of the Declaration of Independence and the
U.S. Constitution, are displayed in the Rotunda of the National Archives in Washington, D.C.

CHAPTER SIX

The Bill of Rights and What It Protects

Below is the text of the Bill of Rights, along with a brief description of each amendment in *italics*. For more than two centuries, legal scholars have disagreed on the exact meaning of many of the amendments. In fact, legal experts have spent entire careers analyzing the meaning of single phrases in the Bill of Rights.

AMENDMENT ONE: Congress shall make no law respecting an establishment of religion, or **prohibiting** the free exercise thereof; or **abridging** the freedom of speech, or of the press; or the right of the people peaceably to assemble, and to petition the government for a **redress** of **grievances**.

Americans are guaranteed freedom of worship, freedom of speech, and freedom of the press (newspapers and other media). Americans are also guaranteed the rights to hold protest meetings and to ask the government to deal with their complaints.

AMENDMENT TWO: A well-regulated militia, being necessary to the security of a free state, the right of the people to keep and bear arms shall not be **infringed**.

Arms means guns. This amendment guarantees that the federal government cannot interfere with the right of Americans to own firearms.

The Bill of Wrongs?

Lawyers, judges, and scholars have argued heatedly about the meaning of the Bill of Rights. The meaning of the Second Amendment—the right to bear arms—has been in great debate. Does it mean that a person can own any kind of firearm, including assault weapons? Should people have to go through a background check before they can buy guns? Should states and cities be allowed to make their own rules about gun ownership, even though the Bill of Rights guarantees the right? Should there be a new amendment outlawing gun ownership altogether? Americans have argued about these issues for many years.

Some people feel strongly that the Second Amendment gives Americans the right to own and use guns responsibly.

The Supreme Court and Freedom of Speech

The Supreme Court of the United States is the highest court in the land. A big part of its job is to review cases about the U.S. Constitution and its amendments. The Supreme Court has made some important decisions about the freedom of speech, which is guaranteed in the First Amendment. In the 1942 case *Chaplinsky v. New Hampshire*, the Supreme Court ruled that personal insults and threats are not part of the freedom of speech. This is because they are "fighting words" and are likely to cause violence.

On the other hand, the 1971 case *Cohen v. California* involved a young man who wore a jacket with a swear word on it. The Supreme Court ruled that this man *was* protected by the First Amendment. This is because the swear word was not directed against another person. The jacket was not likely to cause a fight.

THE BILL OF RIGHTS AND WHAT IT PROTECTS

AMENDMENT THREE: No soldier shall, in time of peace be quartered in any house, without the consent of the owner, nor in time of war, but in a manner to be prescribed by law.

This amendment protects Americans from having their homes used or taken by the military.

AMENDMENT FOUR: The right of the people to be secure in their persons, houses, papers, and effects, against unreasonable searches and seizures, shall not be **violated**, and no warrants shall issue, but upon probable cause, supported by oath or affirmation, and particularly describing the place to be searched, and the persons or things to be seized.

This amendment protects Americans from mistreatment by police and other government authorities. Police must have "probable cause," or some evidence of wrongdoing, before arresting people or searching their homes.

AMENDMENT FIVE: No person shall be held to answer for a capital, or otherwise infamous crime, unless on a presentment or indictment of a grand jury, except in cases arising in the land or naval forces, or in the militia, when in actual service in time of war or public danger; nor shall any person be subject for the same offense to be twice put in jeopardy of life or limb; nor shall be compelled in any criminal case to be a witness against himself, nor be deprived of life, liberty, or property, without **due process** of law;

The First Amendment grants Americans the right to gather in protest of government policy. When police arrest protestors, the Fourth Amendment states that there must be evidence of wrongdoing and that no mistreatment should occur.

nor shall private property be taken for public use, without just compensation.

This amendment protects the rights of people accused of crimes. For example, many movies and TV shows feature people "taking the Fifth Amendment," or remaining silent in court. This refers to the section stating that a person does not have to "be a witness against himself." The "due process of law" section requires the American court system to follow fair rules.

AMENDMENT SIX: In all criminal prosecutions, the accused shall enjoy the right to a speedy and public trial, by an **impartial** jury of the state and district wherein the crime shall have been committed, which district shall have been previously ascertained by law, and to be informed of the nature and cause of the accusation; to be confronted with the witnesses against him; to have compulsory process for obtaining witnesses in his favor, and to have the assistance of counsel for his defense.

People accused of crimes have a right to a fair trial, including a trial by a fair-minded jury.

AMENDMENT SEVEN: In suits at common law, where the value in controversy shall exceed twenty dollars, the right of a trial by jury shall be preserved, and no fact tried by a jury, shall be otherwise re-examined in any court of the United States, than according to the rules of the common law.

Americans have a right to a trial by jury in certain federal court cases.

Ignoring the Amendments

Learned Hand, a famous judge, said, "Liberty lies in the hearts of men and women. When it dies there, no constitution, no law, no court can save it." At times, Americans have forgotten or ignored the Constitution and its amendments. For example, the amendments guarantee the rights to due process, a public trial, and an impartial jury. Yet in the 1800s and early 1900s, thousands of African Americans were accused of crimes and lynched—murdered by mobs—without being given a trial.

AMENDMENT EIGHT: **Excessive** bail shall not be required, nor excessive fines imposed, nor cruel and unusual punishments inflicted.

Bail is money people pay to stay out of jail until their trial. This amendment protects accused and convicted people from being charged too much bail or being punished too harshly.

AMENDMENT NINE: The enumeration in the Constitution, of certain rights, shall not be construed to deny or disparage others retained by the people.

The people have other basic rights besides those mentioned in the Constitution and the Bill of Rights.

AMENDMENT TEN: The powers not delegated to the United States by the Constitution, nor prohibited by it to the states, are reserved to the states respectively, or to the people.

Any powers that the Constitution does not grant to the U.S. government—or deny to the states—belong to the states or to the people.

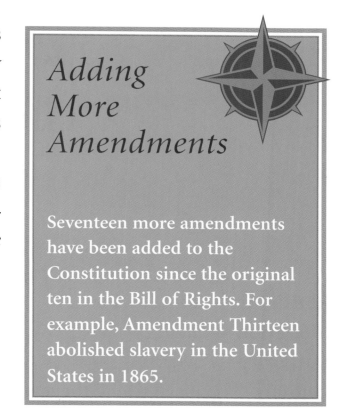

Adding More Amendments

Seventeen more amendments have been added to the Constitution since the original ten in the Bill of Rights. For example, Amendment Thirteen abolished slavery in the United States in 1865.

Glossary

abridging—Taking away.

alteration—Change.

authority—Power.

capital—The place where the laws for a nation or state are made.

colonies—Settlements built by a country beyond its borders.

congress—A body of lawmakers.

constitution—A basic framework of government.

convention—A big meeting.

creed—A set of basic beliefs.

delegates—People who act for other people.

due process—Legal proceedings carried out according to established laws and principles.

entitled—Deserving of.

excessive—Beyond what is normal; extreme.

federal—Relating to the national or central government.

grievances—Complaints.

impartial—Fair; not favoring one side over another.

infringed—Broken, interfered with.

majority—A number that equals more than half the total.

objection—A reason to disagree with something.

opponents—People who are against something.

prohibiting—Forbidding; not allowing.

rebel—To act against authority; to disobey.

redress—An apology; making something right.

violated—Broken; harmed.

Timeline

1607—England settles Virginia, its first American colony

1733—England establishes Georgia, the last of its thirteen American colonies

1760s—Britain tries to tax the colonists; Americans protest

1775—Americans begin fighting the Revolutionary War to break free of British rule

1776—**July 4:** American leaders issue the Declaration of Independence

1783—Americans win the Revolutionary War and achieve independence

1787—The Constitutional Convention creates the U.S. Constitution

1788—**June 21:** The U.S. Constitution goes into effect wh[en] New Hampshire becomes the ninth state to ratify it

1607   *1776*   *1788*

1789—June 8: James Madison presents a bill of rights to the U.S. House of Representatives
September 25: The U.S. House and Senate approve the Bill of Rights
November 20: New Jersey becomes the first state to ratify the Bill of Rights

1790—Rhode Island becomes the thirteenth and last of the original states to ratify the Constitution

1791—December 15: The Bill of Rights takes effect with Virginia's ratification

1941—Bill of Rights Day (December 15) is established as a holiday

1988—Americans celebrate the two hundredth anniversary of The U.S. Constitution

1991—December 15: Americans celebrate the two hundredth anniversary of the Bill of Rights

1791

1941   *1991*

Further Information

B O O K S

Horn, Geoffrey M. *The Bill of Rights and Other Amendments*. Milwaukee: World Almanac Library, 2004.

Rivera, Sheila. *The Bill of Rights*. Edina, MN: ABDO and Daughters, 2004.

Santella, Andrew. *James Madison*. Minneapolis: Compass Point Books, 2003.

Taylor-Butler, Christine. *The Bill of Rights*. Danbury, CT: Children's Press, 2007.

Teitelbaum, Michael. *The Bill of Rights*. Chanhassen, MN: The Child's World, 2005.

WEB SITES

For information on the Constitution and the Bill of Rights from "Ben's Guide to U.S. Government for Kids":
http://bensguide.gpo.gov/6-8/documents/constitution/background.html

The December 15 entry in the Library of Congress "Today in History" series focuses on the Bill of Rights:
http://memory.loc.gov/ammem/today/dec15.html

This National Archives site provides simple background information about the Bill of Rights and George Mason's role in its creation:
http://www.archives.gov/national-archives-experience/charters/bill_of_rights.html

A brief biography of James Madison provided by the White House:
http://www.whitehouse.gov/history/presidents/jm4.html

Bibliography

The Bill of Rights and Beyond, 1791–1991. Washington, DC: Commission on the Bicentennial of the U.S. Constitution, 1991.

Labunski, Richard. *James Madison and the Struggle for the Bill of Rights*. New York: Oxford University Press, 2006.

Levy, Leonard W. *Origins of the Bill of Rights*. New Haven, CT: Yale University Press, 1999.

Monk, Linda R. *The Bill of Rights: A User's Guide*. 3rd ed. Alexandria, VA: Close Up Publishing, 2000.

Patrick, John J. *The Bill of Rights: A History in Documents*. New York: Oxford University Press, 2003.

Schwartz, Bernard. *The Great Rights of Mankind: A History of the American Bill of Rights*. New York: Oxford University Press, 1977.

Index

Page numbers in **boldface** are illustrations.

About the Author

Dennis Fradin is the author of 150 books, some of them written with his wife, Judith Bloom Fradin. Their book for Clarion, *The Power of One: Daisy Bates and the Little Rock Nine*, was named a Golden Kite Honor Book. Another of Dennis's well-known books is *Let It Begin Here! Lexington & Concord: First Battles of the American Revolution*, published by Walker. Other recent books by the Fradins include *Jane Addams: Champion of Democracy* for Clarion and *5,000 Miles to Freedom: Ellen and William Craft's Flight from Slavery* for National Geographic Children's Books. Their current project for National Geographic is the *Witness to Disaster* series about natural disasters. *Turning Points in U.S. History* is Dennis's first series for Marshall Cavendish Benchmark. The Fradins have three grown children and five grandchildren.